green

PAUL MOOREHEAD

green

POEMS

BREAKWATER
P.O. Box 2188, St. John's, NL Canada A1C 6E6
WWW.BREAKWATERBOOKS.COM

A CIP catalogue record for this book is available from Library and Archives Canada

ISBN 9781778530470

Cover Design: Rhonda Molloy
Page Layout: Beth Oberholtzer, Oberholtzer Design Inc

We acknowledge the support of the Canada Council for the Arts.

We acknowledge the financial support of the Government of Canada through the Department of Heritage and the Government of Newfoundland and Labrador through the Department of Tourism, Culture, Arts and Recreation for our publishing activities.

PRINTED AND BOUND IN CANADA.

Breakwater Books is committed to choosing papers and materials for our books that help to protect our environment. To this end, this book is printed on a recycled paper and other sources that are certified by the Forest Stewardship Council®.

MIX
Paper | Supporting responsible forestry
FSC® C103567

Canada Council for the Arts | Conseil des arts du Canada
Canada
Newfoundland Labrador

for Chandra

contents

cracking amber

Once a kid who probably snared lightning
bugs in jars, I might now say, "Stay as you are,

just a little forever longer," as though amber
does any good for the fly. Green as you are,

you won't settle among the fossils. Who
could find stillness so impossible as you? Are

you aware of those chancy mitoses, of unknotting,
of quickening as unstoppably as you are?

Become, then, unmoored, become some more.
Get flying, defiant of that amber. As you are.

Refusal in Calligraphy

Restless as a cricket on a rose,
I quit attempting cursive

the instant they let me.
Elegant words left behind, life

scribbled out before me.
I vanished from Sunday school

before I could remember
doing it. In what may be my

creation myth, my parents left
Belfast, green-soaked Belfast,

lately red-scrawled. Enough
keening, disappearings. Even

toddlers know that No!
is the kindest word, so long

as you write it ten feet tall,
carry it like an Armalite.

carcinize

Evolution keeps imagining
crabs, Monet without the cataracts.

She's re-envisioned eyes
now and then, given flight

a few batty or buggy whirls. Genius
revisiting her subjects, or a

hack with but few ideas? Doesn't
she also dabble in the rogue

cell that leaves one no
better than a Pollock,

thin, butter-spattered, infiltrated?
However useful carapaces,

however pragmatic her caprice,
she probably never intended her

-mit crabs residing in bottle caps,
in shattered lightbulbs' screws.

SPUDUARDO, COME HOME

This is a peace-but
-at-what-price scenario: hush

echoes among these drowsy books
like a one-man heart string

ensemble, absent chaos
wisping in my ear. Some ghosts

flee a hundred years after the famine,
but some lassies are just gone

now, and I'm left sinking in the armchair
with McCabe, or maybe Joyce,

for want of some tale half
better. Waiting on that rhapsodic revenant,

her roaring kisser.
Wondering how, for all her mother's

many bloods, still she sanguinely
ends up with my wee potato face.

thought experiment i

Even the lions among us like a good box.
And nobody but nobody sees into this one.
But what gets my back up — or not —
is sharing space with my own poisoned

corpse. Now we are cozy-cozy with death,
meeting close as whiskers now and again.
But the pharaohs lied about the abundance
of snacks, and I'd miss my naps in the sun.

Still, I'm not opposed in principle
to playful murders at random for the sake
of filling hungry . . . minds. I ask only
that I be kept well clear of philosophic

undergraduates. And, if needed after
I am observed, do find me a nicer box.

Dún Aonghasa

Is some god — forgotten, lingering —
meant to provide inspiration when I drop
by a place such as this? I did not
make the rock-footed climb yesterday,
lashed with rain as that day was.
Today the path is sun-favoured.
The sky boundless. But near the edge
of the cliff, I can think only of bodies.
How many? How many beneath
this memoryless surf? All I've lugged
up here is a slab of paper. Not stones
for some chieftain's whim. To defend
against whom, exactly? No Roman century
or Greek tragedy ever ventured so far.
Acrophobia kindly keeps me from the edge.
At first. But look, I'm crawling, then laid
on belly, now looking over, only face
and fingertips above the Atlantic.
Could any man survive the drop
of so many warrior's paces? Now
I'm verdant with the vertigo and the void
calls me as insistently as any man.
But I'll not accept the charges.
Not today. They were bad Bronze

Age bastards back then, with little regard
for workplace safety. Even they couldn't
fight this deep that can't be fought. Standing
back now, breathing in at last, blood raging
in my eardrums.

the tricks of the albatross

Imagine being
so good at flying
that you can sleep mid-soar.
Or so good at sleeping.
Me, I'm exposed
like a nerve and can't even see
a tangle of blue hurricane-spun
bedsheets in the dryer
without becoming
a cloud of sparks,
an ill-fitting volcano,
just a little guy gnashing
the world like it's all
sticky fridge door handles
and barked
shins — the whole thing.
It's not, of course.
It's a knot, of course.
It's a mariner's knot, of course,
and billows and tells and tempests
and horizons.
And I could show you
if I'd unclench my sooty eyes.
But most days I'm just awed
at either of the albatross's tricks.

«Le silence de reverse» and the flying of charms

My haunted fortune to never was a young poet
gnashing glibly at the fraying of rainbeaux
while undergraduate belles, tresses yellow
or read, query clever and moon hazy
over genius flashing and flying barbe,
pointed versing, not for the crush of ears,
rather scribbling in the mirror after meanings
luminous, perpetual, as yet unflown.

My luck now to hold this baby aloft,
to have this scruff she explores to love
through greying bristle with tiny graspings,
to see sky in the lass, and brass in her eye.
Wrote now a half poem for her, imagined:
ever was an old poet for a half life, half read.

Learn the Bones

Bloodless on brushed steel sky,
we dissect his blemishes. Tattoo
too faded to teach us much.
Bypass graft and whatever beats
that bought him. Large hands,
still holding percussion's scars:
now, stripped of prints
and callous, they resemble the guts

of a piano. Men succeed. Here's how: Guns.
Nooses, and other embraces.
Altitude, and the stop at the bottom.
Imagine that gutsy symphony of me.
Imagine another lesson of this, not the how
of *l'un problème vraiment sérieux*,
but the why not? Yes, why not?

Learn the bones, just don't become them.
This man, no longer
a problem, did he exit on his own
brume? Impatient for the live
tragedies, not this stiff
theatre stuff, still we sweat this cool
relic-scented lab. I'm keeping busy.
Bones and facts hush my fractured
voices. Permitting silence, for once.

waiting for votto

Sometimes there's a ball game,
if you're lucky. And you can buy
a good seat, first base side
a few rows back, even at game time,
if all you need is a single.
My first time at Wrigley;

having already been to Fenway
a few times, I suppose I can die
happy now. The woman who sells me
a thick Cubs hoodie between innings
smiles knowingly: I'm underdressed
for the spring evening. But I'll probably
survive. The cold and the April
stakes haven't kept the crowds away.
But the seats next to me are empty,
nobody to slide into conversation
with. Unusual at a ball game.

My scorecard keeps me company
of a fastidious sort, one man after
another in the box. Only now
do I see it's already out of hand.

But you know how *Hamlet* ends,
and you stick around for the duel
anyway. You never know

what might happen man to man.
But when it's this lopsided, look
around: bricks and ivy, the outfield
is a calm green sea from here.

I'm near enough to see the runner
say something to Votto on his way
back to the bag after a hit.
Votto faces away from me. What
does he reply? Anything? Surely
something: it's Votto. But what?
Maybe anything. Life. Chess.

Anything other than this: sixty
feet six inches, four bases,
the changeup, ending where you begin.

Then it's over. Nothing much happened,
I admit. That's not a problem:
what matters hardly happens at all.
The next day's meetings end too late
for me to catch another game.
So I change into yesterday's hoodie,
and go to Giordano's instead,

ordering beer and a monument
of cheese and dough and pepperoni.
I've brought a novel, which does the talking

while I try to eat it all. And I give it a crack
but the box seems inevitable
when I ask for it. I leave a good tip,
more for the quiet than the service.

The walk outside is cold,
but that isn't so bad. I've my flight
home in the morning. Flying

always wears me out. I'd take the walk
every time, rather than that.
Eventually I'm back at the hotel.
Suddenly weary, I step

into the elevator. The door closes,
but is waved open by an arm burly
enough for a corner spot. A man steps
in, an employee of the hotel, and looks
me up and down. He sees my hoodie,

the newness on it but also the logo,
thinks a moment, and decides
that I am perhaps worth some chatter.

— What you got there, pizza?
gesturing at the box in my hands.
— Yeah. And then, feeling the weight,

I continue — You know, you really
can't finish off one of these deep
dish numbers on your own.
He nods his agreement. The elevator

arrives at my floor. Gravely,
as though he has just cracked
open a pyramid, learnt its secrets,
he says — Not responsibly.

X

Boys and Giants

Give us the future.
We've had enough of your past.

— Michael Collins

It's a tamed green here, less grand
than the evergreen titans I know.
An army truck knocks down
the road, soldiers in the back dancing
sombrely with their machine gun partners.

My parents mustn't like me too well,
sending me to Belfast in '78. I'm seven,
a meagre seven, and army men seem cool.
I don't know about Parnell or Collins,
centuries of cold pharaonic business.

Meanwhile, in Seattle, my parents gape
at the boy king's treasures, on display
for the wage-bound. I'd have liked
to see the mummies: did you know the little
ones are cats? That there are organs

in the jars? But Ulster is okay too,
even if I haven't been to Giant's Causeway
yet. I will see King Tut someday:
disco beats, jazzy sax, sarcophagus,
Steve Martin dancing wildly.

Grandfathers I: John Moorehead

He taught maths. Died
when I was small, before he ever
met me. What little I know of him
is smoke. I visited Belfast in '97,
and even then you couldn't
so much as say hello but a cigarette
found its way in between your fingers.
In the years after the war, there must
have been more smoke in the air
than oxygen. More laughter
than poems. A coronary. No way
for a king who taught maths to go.
The same fingers as held his chalk
held his cigarettes. And the smoke?
I like to think he didn't only inhale
then exhale. Wouldn't he have thought
the spirals upward from the ember?

second strike in chicxulub

Waiting on a second
strike. Ask the *albertosaurus*,
the *apatosaurus* what aftermath is like,
in this crater where I used to live.
A rainbow's worth of pulverized metal
still dusts down. Who doesn't love
a meteorite? Ask the *albertosaurus*,
the *apatosaurus*. The mineral stubbornness.
The tantrum of impact. So small
by the time it burned and screamed
its way through red sky, the same air
that fills my own lungs. So small,
but devastation like I never saw.
All this from a little smack, a kiss
on our calculable orbit from a speck
with its own secret trajectory.
Ask the *albertosaurus*, the *apatosaurus*.
See that scintillating streak above us?
We know what's coming, only we don't
know who. We can't wait.
Hardly feels like an extinction event at all.

JADE JAWS

This guy is just a guy
in green body paint
and I rampage at eight
better than some bodybuilder
who can barely upend a pickup.
I smash tanks,
leap mountains, bounce
bullets off my emerald
hide. Pulverize everything
around me. But it will be a while
before CGI electroshocks such marvels
to life. For now, this CRT
transforms my living room
with gamma rays. Most monsters
are given baroque monikers.
But a purple-pantsed atomic
brute gets one lousy syllable
of Latin. Hulk has no time
for poetic discursion. Or pronouns.
Hulk wants left alone.
Hulk wants forgiveness.
Hulk wants puny boy to see
Lou Ferrigno is fucking huge.

the waking cú chulainn

We hadn't any post offices
then, only bogs and flowered
burial mounds. If I had something
to say, when I was at the vanguard
of the chieftains of Ulster, I rode
up to your man, myself,
and invited him to a fair fight
in which he would surely die
by the century.
                                        Each ancient
bean, with her parcels bound
for places I've not heard
tell of, tells me, starry
-eyed as the dewiest cailín,
that this was the cradle
of a rising. But what rose?
And what's this, Béarla
spoken all over? I'm even
doing it myself. But ours
is the fairest tongue hewn
from Babel's stones,
surely.
            It's a fair
likeness, the bronze

looks well on me. Even
if it makes of me
a man more thran than I was.
                                        Ravens
I recall in thirsty routs.
But always they were further
off, later on, after my deeds.
This one now, though, he perches
near enough to be an old friend.
Grateful, perhaps, for so many
full bellies.
                    At the end,
long after the sorrows
and the tilts, the fey
and the queens, only one
question remains for the monks
and their books: I, son
of Lugh, himself chieftain
of the Tuatha Dé Danann, why
haven't I any trousers on, why
aren't I wearing a geansaí?

BRUNCH WITH OWLS IN SILK

Today, I wonder what "how to get
urine out of nice tie" will incite

the algorithm to think of me. Someone
wanted to accessorize her lemon-

shouting sundress for company
on this haze-grey day. Fog eats

snow, and not a lot of people
know that. You have to live where

the climactic accidents are right.
But some days' sky is so yellow

and so blue and so yellow, it cries
out to be adored, to be mopped up.

mass and volume

I am not yet sea-turtle-
years-old when today I learn
                                        that whales
are the loudest animals. Might
have known, though whenever I scream,
face blue and submerged,
whatever I mean
                              is only muffled. Singing
loud as rocket's
roaring ascent. Imagine.
I can't. But I believe.
I believe
        in creatures
large as churches chanting thunder.
Sounds like any old haunting
                                        on the PBS.
Hippies in wetsuits aren't good
microphones, I suppose. Next
they'll be telling me giraffes
have the highest blood pressure
                                            yet never
yell at their kids.
                              Who stresses

the price of unfallen
leaves, anyway?
                                    All we can do
is float
on whatever buoys our weight.

THIS SEASON, NOBODY CAN PITCH TO HIM.

"Nomar!"

I can see him from here
beyond the outfield fence: frenetic
toe-tapping, glove-fiddling, bat-wheeling.
It's all a dance with .400.
Leading off top two, he pulls one
that lands in the crowd
not far from where I sit.

"Nomar!"

The family next to me has a kid,
she's maybe ten, she slouches,
pulls her M's cap low, as if evening
sun is what's luminous in Seattle.
He comes to bat, takes a walk,
fields a popup, smacks a single
into centre. Every time, the kid
gets gloomier. Every time, I cry:

"Nomar!"

He'll split a tendon in his wrist.
Maybe he already has. He'll be traded
for spare parts, you betts.
He will retire. But this season,
that is all impossible. Bottom nine,
he fields a grounder, on to first,
arm like a whip. The kid, she groans.
I cheer.

"Nomar!"

The kid, she can't
take it anymore. Is it a plea?
A koan? A curse? She cannot
know what she says:

"No more! No more!"

In our house Sunday mornings are for the miracle of waffles

Afternoon. Thursday. Above
a light fixture shrouded in stained
glass, rectangles like a Mondrian.
Walls cyan, not sky. On the floor,
my daughter, three-weeks-old,
sleeps as though guilty.
Her sister, age two, on the couch,
fidgets in devotion to a music video.
She calls the drummer
"some kind of animal." Wanting sleep,
peace, solitude, I have bought
this imperfect harmony
with "Bohemian Rhapsody"
as performed by puppets. Before
getting crunchy, the song takes a breath

I am reminded
each girl composed herself
from two halves of nearly nothing

and then, guitar.

all the lights

Precisely what colour is this girl's eye?
I've no idea. But I've looked. I've tried
all the lights available to me: outside
in spring and summer; indoors at all hours;

in dark when she doesn't sleep, her irises
hardly there. No luck. They're tricksy. Dancers,
those eyes. Annuli. Wonders. Flowers. Queries.
Beginning blue, but a midnight not quite

marine looking back at me like her sister.
Now brown, sometimes green. Or her mother's
sun spun hazel. One day in some mirror
might the hue come to rest? Else there's a fair

chance she'll have a son who'll someday wonder
that his mother's eyes dance in the weather.

male hominid in supermarket

Disliking the before
dawn, its air damp and brackish,
I'd have been no good for the hunt,
at persuading some beast, flush
with the wild potential of his own day,
to abandon cover. Gathering
would suit me less, fossicking
for glossy treasures
in the scrub. Growing things?
Even worse! The star-crossed
photosynthetic in my plot
would have but rag
for leaf, be more fit for a jar
canopic than pickle.

So here I am this mauzy
evening, a neon lodestar
guiding me to "chicken"
that could be parrot or wombat
or dodo, for all I know.
The floor in produce
gleaming sickly. This air
-conditioned barrow is verklempt
with everything wanted,

is a presentiment of the midnight
of need that is coming. But
I love my girls. And we're out
of yoghurt and blackberries.

thought experiment II

I'm not so evolved as you might suppose
yourself to be, but I've been *ook*ing
with the gibbon in the next cage, who
overhears lots of things between shock treatments

in the psych lab. They like their chatter there.
He says infinite is a lot of monkeys,
infinite is a lot of time. And I'm only me.
So what are my chances for getting down

even part of just one monologue?
Have you thought this through? Still,
banging away fierce on this thing is sport
of a kind, though less than a swing

on a tire. But instead of aping old Bill,
might I chance on something $!pnorb55

neighbourly squabble

In autumn between the squalls,
I lift a stroller built for two
out the front door. This disagreeable
gaggle of black metal sticks
weighs a fucking tonne.
Spanning the steps between
driveway and me, a spiderweb.
Suspended at three points,
shimmering with all the rain's
spectacles. I know about silk
and steel. But that is pound
for pound. The web's tiny author
sits assiduously at its centre.
Eyeing me up and up and up and up.

Keeling

these two
wash like a grey surf
over dingy tiles' old griefs

with their
shuffling   leeward
I spy only wake and spray

sallow neon
suns and antiseptic winds
won't tell   lurches a step she does

squalling   rolling
together listing slowly at first
then threatening capsize   over she
goes only her hand grips his windbreaker's back
and polyester snaps ultramarine   bends he does
creaks weary as weathered timbers   but then they
come
aright in their gale

and onward
to some horizon I can't
reckon beyond their bowsprit

Lessons in Wild

Nothing outside a Lagrange point
argues with gravity.
Hanging in space
after springing from the balustrade,
like Wile E run out of desert
by a few steps, this cat
is just waiting
for nine point eight
metres per second
per second
to catch up with her.
She's graceless, as cats go.
Who knows how the landing will go,
kinematically speaking? She'd just amble
up the steps
if there weren't,
in her way,
baby gates.
Though my daughter figured out how
to pick the latches on those ages ago.
Still the kid respects those gates,
like an elephant who's yet
to unlearn
a calf's lesson about the unbreakable tether,

to rampage accordingly. When she's ungentle
she gets a swat from the cat, howls
accordingly. Everyone's about to get
a faceful of natural consequences.

ways of knowing

Poems be like, "O! the incandescent aspidistra /
and the lark"
but never do they mention
the sublime skeleton of xylem and phloem,
or the paradox of pressure that makes for lift.

Poems be like, "Hearts, / all alike in their cadences"
but this spills, unspoken, unused:
trabeculae of muscle, daring action potentials,
tragic anoxic ischemia, each silly dysrhythmia.

Poems be like, "Of course galaxies / spiral like
fingerprints"
but they cannot quite say
what that means, whether friction ridges are made
of stardust, how hands might touch dark matter.

Poems be like, "Here is truth, / known without
experiment."
And somehow, you can't say much
about that. Not that nothing's been seen; rather,
sometimes we all require a luminiferous aether.

Science and poetry are, in fact, inseparable

— Jacques Yves Cousteau

SORRY YOU ASKED

Parties inevitably wind up
in kitchens. Can't we just keep
this microwave company
with the smallest talk?
How about this music?
The kitchen's owner sure
digs the '90s. Me too, though
mostly I've a "Flagpole Sitta" mood.

But then you have to ask.
And I, three drinks careless, choose to answer.
"That must be so hard," you assert.

What, the bookish kind of hard?
Don't let anyone tell you
this is for the clever.
Anyone could do this,
if they cared to. Easy as baking.

I get to fix shit
with molecules. Fucking molecules, man.
Sometimes they're basically napalm.
But sometimes they've all the precision
comfort of a sniper's headshot.
Too much for polite conversation?
Too much?

Of course it's too much

paperwork; calls at all hours; fire alarms arising from those souls smoking away their griefs in the stairwell; everybody droning about parking all the time like no body can stand the embrace of five minutes' weather between a bucket seat's heat and the door; paperwork everywhere; managers managing magisterially; committees committing *harakiri* for all of us; the institution instituting shit that belongs in an institution; that windowless office; nurses' notes reading "doctor aware" as though anyone knows what that means; expected to know it all, knowing I know so little; as a matter of policy; paperwork for every last thing or it didn't happen; paper, paper paper paperpaperpaperpaper, none of it wearing poems, not even dreary shaggy verse for the dreary shaggy kids in the fountain.

Of course it's too much. But
whose life isn't too much for the living?

Whose?

Even when it's bad, though,
it's not that bad.
(Except when it's bad.)
By the end, they're little more
than bones and you could play
"Gone, Daddy, Gone"
on their stubborn breaths,
but there's a coda and it's equal

measures tears and laughter and wonder
at how much living
one can do in so few years.

Besides, kids look weird with hair. Don't they?

Grandfathers II: Thomas Howard Goligher, Esq.

An affable old fellow. Robust
cheeks that I find on my girls.
Eyes blue and a bit sad,
the same creases as crown
every smile in my family.
What else I think I know
is myths. A drinker. He fed
my grandmother's little dog
table foods until, fat, she found
her mistress's heel once more.
He built his own boat, costly
in ways that won't add up,
but it never sailed.
He was in the army during the war,
a cook he said, went East,
never spoke of it. Secret dishes
then, meals in myths, in smoke.
I'm a bit deaf, he told me,
not seeming to mind at all. Him,
he fell down the stairs.

smooth

A giraffe's neck has the same
number of vertebrae as a man's.
So what's your excuse for slouching,
rather than reaching?
We had to invent ice cream
for the headaches, and paper for the cut
-throat vandalism of poems,
the ones whispering uneyed in the alleyway,
also the ones who shout. But
don't they all shout!
punctuate, and scrap
like irons?
Steal the creases
that your trousers earn with their dancing
in the gale. That's after
sticky liquid rust on the knees
is improved
by peroxide bubbles.
Smooth ain't all
it's cracked
up to be. Just ask the sky,
when at last you reach it.

the PHYSICS OF INELASTIC COLLISIONS

Temperature: the speed of the random
dance of molecules. In a winter
in Winnipeg, there is none of that.
Today I woke, my Earth not yet spun
out of its own shadow. A sidewalk
described only in eddies of blowing snow.
Entropy: the tendency toward
dishevelment of all things. That is a bus.
Not mine. That number won't even
stop here. Is it fast enough?
I might have puzzled this out, once.
But now figuring feels a tarrying scrawl.
Momentum: the vigour of mass and velocity.
A fraction of that impelling, this yielding
mind and my problem is solved in a dash –
but the bus rushes by my still scattered
brain. Its inertia unbothered. Snow whorls
in the wake, settles its complex
choreography on the street.
Redshift: the evidence that all things retreat.

Brief notes on your possible doom

1. _____ is a crab.
That's cruel to crabs, terrorizes
their bodies. Yes,
they're gross sea bugs, obviously
from some other planet. Still.

2. _____ is inevitable
so long as you believe in DNA,
in error. And you do.
Among even the flat earthers
and antivaxxers, no one denies entropy
or embraces still the homunculus.

3. _____ is funny.
Yes, funny ha ha,
in how it can care so little
for how you've abused yourself.

4. But _____ is you,
the you gone wrong that we all fear,
eats you from inside, knows
all your bullshit.

5. But a _____ cell isn't you.
It's been corrupted
by typographical errors that maim
intention like a shotgun.

6. Nobody cures _____.
That is the result,
perhaps, of complex negotiations
between the disease and the chemo.

7. Chemo is careful
poisons. Nobody likes hearing
such truths. Nobody
likes hearing magic words like _____.
Mere vibrations invite
catastrophe. Probably.

Dads and Giants, an Apologia

Morning silvers the pools
of this boggy reach alongside the highway
and stones larger than a man could shift
are strewn among them,
like the crusts of peanut butter toast
strewn across the morning of our kitchen floor.

The crusts, I know by what tantrum
they got there. But the stones?
Well, I know that too:
a glacier dropped them there,
carelessly. A mountain of ice
so patient it eats mountains
knows more magic than any tall tale
you'll ever hear. Yet I imagine
giants playing blocks with boulders,
neglecting to tidy up after,
rainwater collecting in their footprints.

Which is all to say: why?
Disorder on the scale of a landscape
is the landscape. I'd love a giant
or a glacier in equal measure. So little
that would be, next to how I love you.
Why, then, my fury over crusts?

And all of that is to say . . .
I had something else in mind.
I thought I'd stand you on my shoulders
and lift you far above the fogs that contain us,
show you off among your bright kin
strewn across the sky.

on the occasion of yet another numinous poem

Yes, you're stardust,
dancing stardust.
But stars don't care
any more than you
for the flakes of skin
that preen and waltz
in the windowlight.
That one star, it warms
you, but no more
than it does empty space;
it's the ball of mud
at your feet that embraces
this castoff heat while
you contemplate the upward.
That one star does keep
you from traversing
too far, but out of gravity's
obligation rather than affection.
Even at perihelion
its gaze is eight minutes,
ten seconds away.
Does that seem near
to you, measured against

the remaining sky?
Write your poem. Strut
in the sunlight. That shadow
at your feet is yours alone.

thought experiment III

Could I not corrupt a few souls? Instead
I measure the speed of molecules, let
the hot ones pass this way, the cold ones that.
In service of what? Perhaps I subvert

some priggish rule that predicts disorder
on a scale even I cannot endorse.
That would at least be something undermined.
But there's debate, and some reason I do work

— work! — with my unrelenting sorting.
The idea further curls my horns. Never
did I rebel, nor fall, nor forget the sight
of grace to be of use. Damned Kelvin,

'twas his invocation that fouled me thus.
Thermodynamics willing, I'll see him burn.

Little Known History, Still Canon

Golem grey is hard to print
with constancy, so furious
green is an exigency. A word
of the sort you learn in comics
in the sixties, along with *astonishing*
and *apocalypse*. Transformation
via vocabulary. And Cold War
accidents. Sphinxily
recumbent, playing harmonica
in a bomb test site on a dare,
that beatnik kid needs
rescuing, a lab coat
gets vaporized. Which is all
forgotten while everyone frets
the rampaging. We all change
colour for antiquated reasons.
Beatnik becomes sidekick, monster
battles monsters and trousers.
Goes grey again,
because nineties rather than age,
works Vegas. Finally named: Mr. Fixit.

A sartorial creature, for once.
Problems smashed, sidekick returned.
We could all use all of that.
Green again, of course, always
green, whether brainy or immortal
or movie star. Always the monster.

OH-san!

Cherry blossoms are crowds of pink taking their seats around the morning grass. But this time of year, between rain and summer's race, the quad's only spectacle is undergrads ambling toward classes. In my backpack a lesson plan, a box of chalk. For scribbling obscure formulae, white lines at right angles. Busy imagining today's lesson. Calculus, dull and beauteous. Only at the last moment I notice the two girls in my way. No time to evade this pickle. They introduce themselves, their English a practiced lineup of polite phrases. Their assignment: to ask people on campus if they know any famous Japanese. At first I do not, and ignorance sinks my eyes. But then I find my answer in the green that holds our feet. The name I say, I have only ever seen in print, I have no idea how it's pronounced. Varying my diction randomly, I say it again. Defeated . . . but no, not quite. I stand on my left leg and tuck the right under me, like some famous flamingo. I make loose fists of my hands, place them together left atop right. I stride and bring these hands forward.

Contact. Climbing up
gravity to shared blue sky.
The girls' eyes widen.

TIDE-LOCKED: A ROMANCE

Look down at this great muddy lout
I'm stood on. He dances with you,
but forever sees only one of your faces.
Here's the trouble with gravity:

his relentless greed. You keep twirling,
making the best of it, waxing a smirk,
waning a wink. Sometimes a retrograde
sidestep. Seldom in daylight. Flirting

with the expanse behind you.
Less vast than that down here, but still
a sea and I am awash. Often clouds
obscure my nights, hide you away.

Endless falling, that's all it is.
When you are visible, I don't see
your partner, who leads by virtue of force
alone. One more blessing of looking up.

Green

L'oppresseur ne serait pas si fort s'il n'avait des complices parmi les opprimés eux-mêmes.

— Simone de Beauvoir

Ireland is the land of saints and scholars.

— Various cunts

Now then, what is green? Inexperience, obviously. The treading soft of foot on stone. Change as well, moss and turf growing over stone, a place at the edge of all the maps, absent toponym.

A tongue, an unspellable bramble once stolen, now brawling with my teeth when I learn his points. But the tongue I was born to is a stately queen in conquering grammar. She's marvellously acquisitive, like her marvellous museum, that catalogue of anonymous loot. And despite a queue of asthmatic hiccoughs in her reign, mostly like herself on the page. Myself? On this page I'm a born accomplice, plainly.

What is green? Wee sorry bastards, sadness on us. But no, we're not all Dubliners. We're Corkers. And UnCorkers, obviously. Belfasteners. And Unfasteners, people come loose. Escaping gibbet or famine or trench or car bomb. A whisper in the ear saying *Get out. Get someplace better.* Even if better just means having your boot on some other poor bleeder's neck the once. And if you've a bit more luck, maybe a wisp of sun and a plot wider than a grave. Who wouldn't leg it? Who wouldn't, when the alternative is to stay, when staying is approving of a few yahoos fucking it up for everyone. All that rowing over different spellings of the same godawful boring tale.

Myths, surely. And just as surely we'd have been better off telling ourselves our own tales, not those imported from someplace too dry for a sensible bog or a decent pour. Haven't we tales enough of our own? A journey to all the worlds that can be imagined, the cacophony of the graveyard, an epic in just a day, rebellion against just one beginning and one ending. Haven't we heroes enough of our own? One so proud he'd bend to no queen, so fierce that at his end his foes feared to come near until they first saw the ravens having a go. Though what a good Ulster demigod is doing in a Leinster post office, I don't know. Ach, there I go, thinking in clans and their brawling. And there's the trouble.

What is green? A violence that has knit us since long before the priests and their pearly Latin, the invaders and their hurly-burly dragons. Bad bastards we've been, kicking the holy hell out of one another with fists and spears, Semtex and Armalites. Bogtrotters through and through our sodden souls.

This whiskey that shocks down the back of my throat is a telegraph sparking at gossiping ancestors in the clay, asking in dots and dashes, between the shots and lashes, *What were you thinking?* What were you thinking when you chose to bend and to thank them for it in their own tongue, whoever they were that one century?

What is green? Five hundred nanometres, give or take. The chlorophyll reflecting photons at such wavelengths. Or, in the eye that refracts the photons, the opsins that capture them. The visual cortex that lamps the signals, the poem of mind that turns them into landscape. A landscape of grass growing between all the stones, grass bending soft in the breeze. The grass made of cells, the cells making chlorophyll, the chlorophyll written long ago by genes like a myth.

us monsters

I've this key fob with pouting green face,
hair short and shaggy and frayed as a fuse.

My girl loves this face enough, I worry,
to swallow him whole. She's still living

her origin story, but already knows how
to roar. — What does Hulk say?

—'MASH!!! She's a furious sketch
of him at times, pulverizing

the suggestion of nap time, the wresting
away of a battery, a lightbulb. This giant,

I hope he's a different monster for her
than for me: less irradiated, trousers untattered.

You wouldn't like me when . . . was useful
in my faded back issues. But he's inked

into me still, and makes me a dangerous
character. No, I'd like him to be her choice,

her tool, a pencil she sharpens for villains,
abominations. SMASH!! she'll say, grinning.

LIGHTS OUT

Whip the socks off at four,
witchy arrives at six.
Pterodactyl is sad because
he has no moustache,
is the wisdom from the tub.
Pop! go the bubbles, laugh
like they're dancing.
A buzzing makes
a bee. You'll wing it yet,
touch phalanx
to sky. Stomp!
'til then, so we all mishear.
Pick out your rocket ships,
or else the whales. Stories
sing the outro for the day. But
before we call this adventure, Yes!
daddy want to pick you up.

notes

Cracking Amber and *Dads and Giants, an Apologia* first appeared in *Pinhole Poetry*.

Brunch with Owls in Silk first appeared in *Riddle Fence.*

Waiting for Votto, This season, nobody can pitch to him, and *Oh-san!* first appeared in *Turnstyle: The SABR Journal of Baseball Arts*.

The Waking Cú Chulainn: In the Dublin General Post Office stands a memorial to the Easter Rising of 1916, a bronze by the sculptor Oliver Sheppard, entitled *The Dying Cú Chulainn*.

No cats, monkeys, or demons were harmed in the writing of the *Thought Experiment* poems.

acknowledgements

This book would not have been possible without Chandra Kavanagh. Her love and support, which at times ran to forcing me to leave the house to go write, made these poems happen. Our daughters Moira and Aoife provided much of the inspiration for this book. They are incandescent humans and deserve to have a much better poet writing about them, but Seamus Heaney wasn't available. I hope they'll be proud of their dad anyway.

George Murray was my first poetry teacher, when writing poetry was just something I did to kill time during the pandemic. He is a mentor, friend, and dungeon master. He also edited this book, transforming it through wizardry into something much more coherent and forceful than it was in its first draft.

I am genuinely grateful to Breakwater Books for bringing *Green* to published life. Thanks to Rebecca Rose for taking a chance on an elderly emerging writer and to Rhonda Molloy for her striking and beautiful cover design, and to everyone at Breakwater for their hard work in making my poems into a book that might find its readers.

I am part of the Walk the Line virtual poetry community. The very real support that I have found there has been amazing. Particular thanks to Donna Kane, Paul Robichaud, Joelle Barron, Marilyn Belak, Tanja Bartel, August Bourre, Heather Ramsay, Rhonda Douglas, Lana Crossman, and Shelagh Rowan-Legg.

In 2022–23, I participated in the WritersNL Mentorship Program for Emerging Writers, which is sponsored by the Canada Council for the Arts. Many of the poems in this collection were begun during this program. My mentor, Douglas Walbourne-Gough, is a wonderful poet and a great poetry teacher. It is thanks to Douglas that I learned to trust my own voice on the page and to listen very closely to the sounds of a poem.

As a new poet, the first acceptances of my work for publication were a uniquely valuable encouragement. I am especially grateful to Erin Bedford at *Pinhole Poetry* for her kind words and enthusiasm for my work at this early stage of my life as a poet.

The bartenders at Yellowbelly Brewery and Public House in St. John's might be surprised to know that the guy at the end of the bar was writing poems in his notebook all that time. Many thanks for leaving me to write without a lot of chit-chat, and for pouring that next pint of cream ale without my having to ask.

Paul Moorehead is an emerging writer in St. John's, Newfoundland where he lives with his partner, their two daughters, and a cat who loves snacks. When not writing, he is a pediatrician. His poems have appeared in *Riddle Fence*, *Pinhole Poetry*, and *Turnstyle*: *The SABR Journal of Baseball Arts*. He has an MA in Critical and Creative Writing from the University of Gloucestershire.